50 Ways to FLOURISH AFTER DIVORCE

Patti J. Handy

Copyright 2011 © Patti Handy

For quantity discounts, please contact Patti at Patti.Handy@VanceWealth.com

ISBN 13: 978-0-9824656-3-9

ISBN: 0-9824656-3-7 Library of Congress Control Number: 2014922179
Patti Handy, Valencia, California

To my Mom and Dad,

My Sisters and Brothers,

and dear friends,

who stood by me every step
of the way.

And to my precious son whose
smile and love became my
inspiration.

Dedication

To those seeking peace and happiness, again...

Not only will you survive divorce, you will thrive.

You will find *yourself* again and experience a life of joy and excitement.

Be patient.

It will happen.

Believe it.

My story

I'm going to imagine my story is not much different from yours. It was a lifetime ago--a distant memory, yet crystal clear: the day my then-husband told me he wanted a divorce. At the time, my son was fast asleep and only 18 months old. Thoughts of him flooded my brain, while my heart couldn't bear the pain and shock. It took me a minute to realize that I had stopped breathing. I thought I was going to roll over and wake from a horrible nightmare. Instead, I rolled over and cried, for what seemed forever. I remember thinking "I can't cry anymore, there can't possibly be anymore tears left inside of me." But, there were.

Fast forward a year. Things were better, but tough, with my son being so young. I was juggling work as a single mom to a toddler. I was struggling financially, emotionally and physically. But, I did feel the healing taking place. The first year was difficult because I went through all 'the firsts'. The first holidays, Valentine's Day, Birthday, Thanksgiving, Anniversary etc.

As time marched on, I healed, I grew and then I flourished. I became myself again. That time of healing was necessary. I was healing an emotional wound that had to take its course. Much like healing a physical wound, Mother Nature played a part. No matter how fast I wanted to feel better, I

knew a process had to take place
to be whole again. We

cannot wish a broken leg to heal
quickly, no more than we can wish
a broken heart to heal quickly.
BUT, how we take care of
ourselves during this process plays
a huge role in the end result.
Again, comparing it to a broken leg,
if we jumped around, never rested
and abused our body, the leg
would not heal properly.
Eventually, we would walk again,
but perhaps a bit compromised.
Healing a broken heart follows a
similar path.

Although dreams may be shattered
and life seems impossible, I
promise you that you can not only
survive, but thrive. How can I make

that promise? Because I have been through a devastating divorce that completely rocked my world, yet I am so unbelievably happy today. I know it hurts beyond any pain you've experienced. I completely understand, and yet, I can tell you, without a doubt, your life will be amazing again. If you allow it.

It will take time and the healing won't happen overnight. But, it will happen. The purpose of this book is to help you on many levels in turning your life around. I will share what worked, and didn't work, for me and share tips and tools to help you heal and move forward. My hope is that this book will help you heal properly. My hope is that this book gives you hope, courage and the tools to get through one of the most difficult challenges in life. You are not alone in this, yet it is up to you to take care of yourself. Be good to you and know that life will be much better.

50 Ways to *Flourish*

After Divorce

In no particular order, I've listed 50 important steps you can take to move forward and heal. Be patient with yourself and know this is a journey and a process, much like everything else in life. These all worked for me and I know they will work for you. Some days, some of these suggestions will resonate more with you. Some will really hit home one week and a different suggestion may get you thinking two weeks later.

Here we go...

1. Lean on family.

This suggestion seems like a 'no-brainer,' but you would be surprised at how many people just don't reach out to family. There is nothing like the unconditional love and support of family. Parents, sisters, brothers or any other family member you feel comfortable with. They all love you and want to see you happy again. Even if you haven't spoken in a while, reach out to them and ask them for help. If it weren't for my family, I wouldn't be where I am today. I have the greatest parents, two amazing sisters, who happen to be my best friends, and two awesome brothers. I am truly blessed with my wonderful family. If you are lucky enough to have family close by, spend extra time with them. Have dinner together, catch a movie or just take a walk. Talk and unload what is weighing heavy in your heart. Process this time with the love and support of family and you will feel the healing taking place. If family is not close by, take advantage of technology and Skype with them, or just get on the phone. I understand that sometimes reaching out is difficult, but you need to do this.

2. Lean on friends.

Lean especially on those that have gone through a divorce. Every one of my friends helped me in some capacity, but those that had gone through the same emotional roller coaster, understood it better. Share your emotions with both men and women, as they each have great and different perspectives. Don't be shy about asking for help. Your friends love you and want to see you happy again. As with your family, get out of the house and grab dinner or a movie with friends. Talk through your anger, fears, sadness and challenges.

Unfortunately, to your surprise, you may find that some of your friends abandon you. It might be because they are/were friends of your ex, or maybe they are just uncomfortable with your pain. For whatever reason, this may happen.

New friends will come into your world and enrich your life more than you realize. You may meet them at your place of worship, in a class, at your kid's school or through work. Embrace the new relationships and release the old.

3. Exercise.

Do something. Anything! This was huge for me on many levels. First, exercise is one of the first prescribed remedies for those who show signs of depression. The endorphins and chemical changes that you experience with exercise are vital to the healing process. Second, exercise helps you feel better about yourself, which is crucial during this difficult time of self-awareness. When you look better, you feel better about yourself and self-esteem is lifted. Third, exercise also relieves stress and anxiety, which, as you know, are at an all-time high now. In addition, regular exercise helps with a good night's sleep. And, we all know how our sleep is disrupted during this challenging time! Find something you really enjoy doing, so exercise doesn't become a chore. Take a class for more social interaction, which is good for you too.

If you haven't exercised in a while, you may want to get a clearance from your doctor. Also, consider hiring a personal trainer, which not only helps with the training program itself, but also keeps you accountable. Knowing that you can't skip out on an appointment keeps you on track.

4. Take vitamins.

I can't stress enough how important it is to take very good care of yourself right now. I am not a nutritionist or dietician, just a person who's been in your shoes. Emotionally, things are difficult, which makes your physical well-being all that more important. You probably aren't eating as well as you should, so vitamin supplements should be an integral part of your daily routine. Seek advice from a medical, holistic or homeopathic doctor for guidance. A nutritionist or dietician is a great source of information as well. You absolutely must take good care of your body!

If you don't know where you start, ask your friends or family for a referral. Oftentimes, you can get great advice from the staff at a reputable vitamin store.

More is not better, so don't feel you have to take a medicine cabinet full of vitamins. Go get good advice!

5. Eat well.

Eating was the last thing I wanted to do, but I felt terrible when I didn't. Cooking wasn't high on my "fun" list either, especially for one. Actually, it was 1 ½ for me, but still not something I wanted to do. This goes along with the exercise and taking vitamins routine. You will be much better equipped to deal with the emotional issues when you feel stronger and healthier physically. Keep it simple but force yourself to eat well. Home cooking is generally healthier and easier on the budget, but treat yourself to a nice restaurant when you can. Have it delivered if you're more comfortable eating at home.

Be sure to include a healthy balance of fruits and vegetables, along with protein.

If you need some suggestions, again, seek the help of a nutritionist or dietician.

6. Find a new hobby or revisit an old hobby.

Bowling anyone? Golf? Tennis? Photography? I took up martial arts. It was a complete mental escape for that one hour I was kicking, punching and being thrown to the ground. Although my body was being pushed to the limit, my mind was on vacation--something I needed desperately. It felt so good when I was able to turn my brain off and it seemed that getting completely engaged in a physically demanding sport help me do that. It wasn't pretty, but I felt stronger and more confident. Speaking of "not so pretty", I also got back to horseback riding. Something powerful happens when you put on a pair of cowboy boots!

Whatever it may be, find something that helps you escape the daily grind. If your hobby includes a friend, all the better. The social interaction is good for you, and like having a personal trainer, keeps you accountable. You're more likely to stick with it if you have a partner in crime.

7. Get regular massages.

Personally, this is my all-time favorite. What could be better than being pampered? Besides, it has been proven that regular massages have many health benefits. Did I mention it feels good? If massages aren't in the budget, consider trading services, or bartering. Many people trade services of all kinds. If you can't commit to an hour, squeeze in a half hour massage. At minimum, have your feet and hands massaged on a regular basis. There are salons that offer just that service and it's much more affordable. Go ahead, you deserve it.

Find a friend, and do each other's nails. Whatever your budget, you can find a way to pamper yourself.

8. Pray.

Prayer helped me tremendously. It still does. There were times I got down on my knees, and then there were the times I was laying on the floor. Sometimes, I prayed while I was walking or just sitting outside.

If you don't believe in God, pray to whatever higher power you believe in. If you do believe in God, find a church home or place of worship. You may need to visit a few different churches before you find one that feels right. Being part of a worship community is a wonderful, supportive, safe place to be.

Once you find a worship home, consider getting involved with one of the ministries or groups. Pray for strength, courage and faith. Be still and listen with your heart. Prayers are answered and miracles do happen.

9. Get a physical.

Go to the doctor and get a clean bill of health. Free your mind of worries that something may be wrong.

Sometimes when we aren't feeling our best, our minds can play tricks on us and suddenly we are convinced we have some life-threatening disease. (Maybe that was just me.)

Knowing that we are physically healthy can give us a sense of peace that we are going to be okay. It's just one less thing to worry about.

10. If possible, get a pet.

Although this takes additional work, especially if there is potty training involved, the payoff is great. Animals love us unconditionally and they fill our homes with fun and silliness. They keep us company when we're lonely and kiss us anytime we want...unless you opt for a parrot, in which case I would pass on the kiss.

If you have children, a pet also helps with their healing. We got a lovable toy poodle that we adore. My son has the responsibility of feeding her and doing 'poop patrol'. There's the added benefit of having a pet....teaching your children responsibility.

11. Volunteer.

Doing for others helps you out of your own saddened mindset. Find a food shelter, a homeless shelter, a hospital or organization that is in your community. Take flowers to a convalescent hospital or toys to the sheriff department during the holidays. If you are involved in your house of worship, volunteer in some capacity to give back. Think about a senior center or exploring a nonprofit organization. Can you sing? How about teaching a class in digital photography?

I once heard a story about a gentleman teaching a digital photography class at a senior center. Apparently, the class was in such high demand, there was a waiting list! At one point during the presentation, an older gentleman asked, "Where in the heck do you put the film?" Oh my goodness, I love seniors citizens!

12. Read.

Spend some quiet time reading, just for you. Read self-help, motivational, inspirational, comedy or trashy novels-- whatever helps your mind escape for a bit. Reading takes you to another place and time, at least for a while. If you want to read just to escape, you can do that, too. Learning something new is also empowering and helps with the cobwebs in your mind.

I suggest visiting your library as opposed to buying. If you love the book and intend on rereading it, then by all means, buy it. I really enjoyed reading inspirational material. It helped me with the hope that I seemed to lack and gave me the indication that while my pain and sadness were part of the journey, I wasn't going to feel that way forever.

13. Smile and say

Thank You. When you

smile, even when you don't feel like
it, people smile back. It starts a
reaction (much like the Law of
Attraction) that feels good.

In some way, it reminds you that
there is goodness in this
sometimes crazy world we live in.
Saying "Thank You" shows
gratitude and being grateful is
another way to start this chain
reaction.

14. Give to yourself.

I do not suggest going out and buying a new car or purchasing something major. That will just add to the stress of finances and will be a short-lived thrill! What I am suggesting is that you pamper <u>you</u> during this time.

Treat yourself to a manicure, pedicure or facial. This goes for men or women!

Perhaps once every few weeks or once a month, whatever is comfortable financially. Treat yourself to whatever allows you to escape for a while. Maybe it's a latte at your favorite coffee shop, a walk in the park or just time with friends.

15. Take a painting class.

I tried my hand at watercolor. It helped me laugh. I couldn't draw an apple, or anything else for that matter, but I met some nice people and I was proud of myself for trying something new.

If nothing else, it was a welcome distraction. If painting scares you (which I would completely understand, especially since I've tried it), consider taking a drawing class. Drawing involves just pencil, paper and perspective-- another nice way to mentally escape for a bit.

16. Write in a Journal.

Something happens when you write in a journal. It's very therapeutic and it helps clear the clutter in your mind. Even if it's for five minutes, write something every day. I look back at my journal writing, years later, and enjoy observing the growth. The best way to journal is to just write, without judgment or qualifying.

No filter. Just let your thoughts, hurts, angers, fears, joys, accomplishments, or any other emotions run free. The process helps flush out the feelings and clears the path for healing.

17. Take a dancing class.

Personally, I never did this. If you saw me dance, you would understand why.

To say I have two left feet is an understatement. But, if I could, I would have.

The physical workout will be good for you and the social aspect can be a lot of fun. There are many places that offer these classes for singles, so don't be concerned about going it alone.

18. Learn a new language.

Think about a place you want to visit someday and learn that language.

Perhaps your career could benefit from a second or third language. Besides, you don't want to be in a foreign country without being able to ask where the restrooms are!

This also helps with clearing out the cobwebs that can build as you heal emotionally.

19. Learn to play an instrument.

I learned to play the drums. Although some would say I never learned, I had a blast banging!

My son took lessons with me and as it turns out, he's awesome! We still have the drum set in my home and I'll go "play" occasionally.

Funny thing, my son always comes in and corrects my rhythm. Very cute sometimes, other times, not so much. I also took piano lessons for a while. I have such an admiration for musically talented people. Wish I could say I was one of them...

20. Seek professional

help.
Don't be shy about seeing a therapist. Their knowledge and expertise can be vital to getting you back on track.

I received some wonderful support and guidance from a therapist. Processing my experience with a qualified, objective professional helped me put things in perspective.

Without question, if you feel like you're losing control, seek professional help.

21. Be gentle with yourself.

There will be some good days and then, out of nowhere, a horrible day will smack you upside the head. Understand that the healing is taking place and sometimes you take a step backwards to take two steps forward. Accept that as part of the process.

We, especially women, can be very tough on ourselves. We are expected to maintain the home, the kids, and possibly a job as well.

Although we carry these responsibilities, we must take care of ourselves first. If the house gets

messy or you need to order dinner
in, let it go.

22. Take things one day at a time.

Don't try to figure out everything right now. You don't need to know the details of your future. That will all come together in due time. In the beginning, you may need to take things one hour at a time. That's ok. Allow yourself to just get by for now.

I remember some days I would wake up and have no idea how I would get through the day. So, I just told myself, I need to get through to lunch time... then dinner time. In time, that didn't happen anymore.

Trying to figure everything out can be overwhelming, especially when you are so "raw".

In addition, any decision you make in this vulnerable and sensitive state, probably won't be the best decision.

23. Work in the garden.

Getting down and dirty with the earth can be very calming. Plant flowers with lots of color and aroma. If you don't have a garden, make one. Use pots and beautiful containers if necessary. Try planting herbs that you can use in cooking and enjoy the aroma while they grow.

I loved walking through the garden section of my local home improvement store. The colors, the smells, and the greenery brought a sense of serenity over me.

24. Breathe deeply.

When you find yourself tense, which at this point in your life is often, stop and take five very deep breaths. Inhale through your nose and exhale through your mouth.

Breathe from your diaphragm, not your chest. Watch your belly rise and fall as you breathe. Breathe slowly and evenly.

Believe it or not, this works to help calm you, even in the most anxious of times.

25. Be grateful.

I can almost hear you chuckle at this one. How can I be grateful at a time like this? It's not easy, I'll give you that. But, if you can, find one thing that you are grateful for every day. It will slowly shift your perception from what is wrong in your life, to what is right in your life. It takes practice, but make a very gallant effort and you will reap the rewards.

I keep a "gratitude journal" by my bed. I try to write down three things I am grateful for every night. Whether it's your health, your kids, or just the cup of hot cocoa you just drank, being grateful helps you stay positive.

26. Step back and think about your purpose in life.

This is a heavy one, especially at this time in your life. There is a lot of chaos going on and thinking about a subject as deep as this seems counterproductive.

I would recommend waiting a few months to tackle this, but think about it. Now is the time to think about your life-what makes you happy, how you feel fulfilled, how you give back to the world and what fills your soul.

It may be a new beginning for you that you never stopped and thought about. I was listening to a teleconference years ago and heard a great quote. I don't know who said it originally, but I loved it. He said: *"There are two great moments in your life. One is when you were born; the second is when you figure out why."*

Makes you stop and think, doesn't it? Why do you think you were put here?

You have a special gift to share, as everyone on earth does. So, take some time and think about taking those gifts, talents and skills, and putting them to work.

27. Surround yourself with positive people.

This goes for anyone, divorcing or not. Don't let the negative emotions of others take you further down. Rather, be with those that have a positive outlook on life and can help you by focusing on the future.

Join networking groups or organizations that resonate with you. Hang out with "like-minded" people and you'll find yourself feeling lighter in no time.

Join groups on Facebook or LinkedIn that will inspire you to move forward.

28. Every day, try to find one thing that makes you happy.

This, like being grateful, helps you slowly shift your focus and perception to the good that life has to offer. Think about the love of your children, your family and friends and what gift you offer the world.

Early in process of facing life as a single mom, I thought often about the past and "our time together", which did not make for a good day. Slowly, let go of the past and work toward looking forward. Look at

today and appreciate the love that
surrounds you.

29. Find a way to give back to the world.

This lifts the spirit and fills the soul with happiness. When we give to others, we give to ourselves. Whether it's your time, money or a prayer, giving to others is incredibly healing.

It also helps put into perceptive your present situation. When you see what others are struggling with in life, it oftentimes helps with shifting your thoughts, especially if you feel stuck.

This one may need to be a few months down the road, but think about it as you heal.

30. Dream.

At this time in your life, you probably think that life as you know it is over. It is.

The key phrase here is 'as you know it'. But, life is far from over.

<u>It can, and will, become better than you ever thought possible.</u> Have a dream and believe with all your heart that it can come true.

Albert Einstein once said: "Imagination is everything. It is the preview of life's coming attractions."

Dream big... really big.

31. Believe in yourself.

This can be difficult at first, especially if you didn't ask for the divorce. I want you to sit down and write a list of all your wonderful qualities.

Don't be shy, but brag like crazy. List everything. Then post that list on your bathroom mirror and read it every morning, out loud.

You are amazing. Believe this with every bone in your body.

32. If you have kids, keep them out of it.

Whether the kids are 3 or 30, don't drag them down with all the details of the divorce. It does nothing more than make it more difficult for them and create confusion in their minds. You will probably end up alienating them from you, not your ex. As hurt as you are, keep things very neutral with the kids. I realize how difficult this can be, but try to stay focused on what you are gaining and who you are hurting. You gain nothing and hurt the kids, and yourself. I have seen many relationships where the parents put the kids in the middle and everyone suffers, for no good reason.

33. Consider hiring a life coach.

A life coach can oftentimes help guide you and help you focus in a time when everything seems out of control. They can help bring out the best in you when you can't. A good coach is trained at listening to your agenda and helping you move forward. The coaching sessions are 100% about you and your healing. There is reflection, support, guidance, accountability and more.

A life coach differs from a therapist, so consider both, as they offer different services. My suggestion is to seek help from a therapist in the early stages of your divorce, and

then include a life coach as you
begin to feel more settled.

34. Get out of the house.

Staying home can be very relaxing and feel like a safe haven. I love being home.

But, it's important not to get stuck in the rut of being home. Social interaction is important to our minds, our self-esteem, our self-awareness and overall well- being.

Positive distraction is healthy, and getting out of the house will help you with this.

35. Don't focus on dating.

This one is controversial, but I do have an opinion. I have seen couples out dating before the divorce is final, which, in my opinion, serves only one purpose: to feel desired (and maybe to piss off our ex).

That's a perfectly normal and human need! We all need that, but to jump into the dating scene so early will usually delay your healing.

Like a death, you need to go through the grieving process. If you are still incredibly angry or deeply saddened, what type of dating experience will that be for you? It will probably be very unfulfilling, which in turn, will deepen your anger or sadness.

Take care of you first, heal yourself, and then go out and enjoy the journey of finding someone special.

Besides, you will attract the right person for you when you are the right person for you first! Note: don't fall into the trap of needing someone to make you happy.

I'm not a licensed therapist or psychologist, but I know what did, and didn't work, for me and many others that I have spoken to.

36. Envision your new life.

Write out, in great detail, what your new life looks like to you. Like a roadmap to a future destination, having a plan helps us focus on the end result. Not only does it give our life direction, how else would we know we arrived!

Envision your mission, your goals, where you will be financially, emotionally, physically and spiritually.

What you focus on expands, and the law of attraction plays a part. Be very specific about what the perfect life looks like for you. The more detail, the better.

Some people create vision boards. These are nothing more than large posters with pictures of your life's vision and dreams. Simply grab a bunch of magazines and cut out pictures of those things you want. Be sure to put the poster in a location that you can view daily.

The more details, the better. Enjoy the process of envisioning your future and all the health and happiness you will experience.

37. Watch comedies.

As silly as this sounds, laughter does lift the spirits. At a time when sadness seems to dominate your day, a good laugh is a wonderful release.

Some of the older classics are a great option, but grab whatever appeals to you.

With the online movies and TV shows, this should be easy to access.

If you prefer to read, grab a good book that brings on the chuckle.

38. Forgive.

Depending on where you are in the healing process, this may be difficult. It took me a very long time to work through this one. Regardless of what your ex did to you, at some point, you must, for your sake, forgive them. Let me repeat this one: <u>this is for your sake, not theirs</u>. This is letting you "off the hook", not them. They will never know (or care for that matter), if you forgive or don't forgive them.

You must free yourself of this ball and chain that eats away at your spirit. Whether or not it was your decision to divorce, is not the issue here. Remaining angry will ruin your life, not theirs.

I'm not suggesting you push down your anger or deny it. You must feel the feelings. Many so-called spiritual people suggest you shouldn't have "negative" feelings. That's denial and misses a crucial point- that those feelings are where the authentic power is and that our strength, in fact, lies in our vulnerability and our willingness to show up as fully human. You cannot heal what you don't feel. When people access their pain, this is the beginning of their healing. So, feel the pain, the sadness and anger, but then, in time, release it.

Besides, if you don't forgive them and remain in the victim role, your ex has control over you. How's that for motivation?

39. Play.

If you have young kids, or grandkids, play with them. Get on the floor and roll around. Go to the park and swing. Play board games or play dress up.

Allow yourself to be a little silly. Don't worry, nobody is watching. Besides, if somebody is watching, they are probably very envious.

If you don't have kids or grandkids you may want to avoid the dressing up part. You might get arrested.

40. Remember you're not alone.

Just knowing that there are others out there who are feeling exactly how you are feeling, can help.

When I spoke to someone who could totally relate and understand me and my issues, it was wonderful support. It's not that "misery loves company," it was more of "I didn't feel so alone."

41. Value your strength.

There is great wisdom within us, but at a time like this, it tends to hide. You have more intuition, courage and strength than you realize. The hard part is tapping into that wisdom, especially now.

Take 10 minutes every day to find quiet and listen. This may be in prayer, meditation or simply staring into a candle.

You'll be amazed at the strength and courage you uncover.

42. Enjoy a bath.

Most of us have very full days,
going at warp speed to accomplish
all that we need to in one day.

Our responsibilities can be
overwhelming and very stressful.
At the end of the day, try to take 15
to 20 minutes to enjoy a warm
bath.

Let your body sink into the warmth
and quiet of the night, while your
mind slows down. Even if you do
this once a week, it helps ground
you.

43. Take control of finances and debt.

First things first. You must organize your world. If you don't have your papers in one central location, gather everything and put it on the floor. It's time to get organized! Get your bills, mortgage/rent information, legal papers, insurance papers, life insurance information, retirement/401K statements and any other financial documentation you have.

Purchase a small fireproof box that can be locked, and place all this paperwork inside.

Gaining control of your finances will bring you such a sense of empowerment and peace. The reality is that no one cares more about your money than you.

Although the realization of this can be somewhat overwhelming during this difficult time, don't let it scare you. Ask for help from friends and family.

44. Slow down or you'll trip.

Being on your own now brings added responsibilities and time constraints. To keep up with everything, we tend to speed up to get it all done.

After a while, burnout happens, which hurts everyone around us, mostly ourselves.

Please try to slow down and pace things in order of priority. The reality is that some things won't get done and that is perfectly acceptable!

Remind yourself that you are a human being and not Wonder Woman or Superman.

45. Don't try to be everything to everyone.

Women especially fall into this dilemma. Set your boundaries and learn to say "no" when necessary. Over-scheduling or over-committing yourself to others, and their needs, will just add to the overload you are experiencing.

Your friends and family will understand and accept you, regardless of your ability to help them. Whether it is at work, your child's school or personal friends, keep your outside commitments in check, which will allow you to take care of you.

I, too, tried to be everything, at all times, to my son. This not only was an impossible task, it was unhealthy for both my son and I.

Playing super woman (or man) only burns us out and does nothing to help us heal.

46. De-clutter and organize.

De-clutter everything from your closets to your office space. Gather old clothes and shoes and donate them to a women's shelter or other service organization. Purging the old "stuff" can be therapeutic in itself.

Organize important papers, bills, legal documents and insurance information. Creating an organized environment that is clutter free can give you a sense of calm and control.

Chaos breeds more chaos. This is especially important in your home, as this is a place you generally find peace.

47. Allow yourself to cry.

Crying is a release that must happen. If you stifle your true emotions, you aren't allowing yourself the chance to heal. Let yourself "feel fully", without judgment. The shower is a safe place to just let go and cry.

I know some of you are thinking, "Umm, hellooo, I can't stop crying!"

Yes, I know. I remember. But, if you're one to hold it in, don't. Find yourself a quiet, private place and let it out.

48. Find your "self" again.

Spend time getting to know who you are again. Oftentimes, we women tend to put others' needs ahead of our own, which over time can disconnect us from ourselves.

Spend some quiet time revisiting what you are about.

This may involve getting together with friends, taking the classes I mentioned earlier, or just having quiet time to reflect. Journaling also helps.

Personally, I got lost in my marriage. I take total responsibility for it, so I have no one to blame but myself.

It wasn't until several years after my divorce, I found "me" again. And, more importantly, I haven't lost her! Well, except when I have chocolate.

49. Never give up hope.

During this time of emotional exhaustion, it can seem like all hope is lost. Despair can be overwhelming, and it can take over your every thought.

This is the time to reach out and ask for help, especially from friends and family. Know that this is a normal emotion and that it will pass with time and help.

If you ever feel like you are losing control of your emotions, please seek professional help. As I mentioned earlier, working with a professional can be extremely beneficial during this difficult time. I know it helped me!

I promise you, as someone who has walked your walk, life will be wonderful again. Never, ever give up hope.

50. Lastly, and most important: allow all of the above suggestions into your life, without feeling guilty.

I cannot stress enough how vitally important it is to give back to yourself, without feeling like you are being selfish. Without your heart and soul feeling at peace and balanced, there is no way you can bring that to your family. We simply cannot give to others that which we do not have ourselves.

One last thought...I guess this should have been number 51... In this volatile and raw stage in your life, try your best not to be "reactive" to your situation and/or to your ex. The more you become proactive, the more empowered you are.

You don't have control over his/her actions, but you can control your behavior. Focus on taking care of YOU and your kids. I realize this may be tough, especially now, but just be aware of this dynamic.

I hope these suggestions will help you on your journey to healing and empowerment. As I mentioned earlier, your life will be amazing again. You must put forth the effort

to take care of yourself and allow
the journey to take its course.

Now, go out and THRIVE!

I want to share an added resource
you may enjoy...

About the Author

It wasn't until Patti went through a divorce, did she fully appreciate the financial education her parents taught her at a young age. As a child, she learned how to earn her own money, save it and invest it wisely. Little did she know, this would prove to be an invaluable blessing later in life.

With her 18-month-old son by her side, she suddenly found herself terrified, overwhelmed and emotionally distraught. Through the darkness, she knew she would be okay, understanding she had the money skills to take care of herself, and her son.

This has been the catalyst to follow her passion of empowering and educating women in their financial journey. Understanding that money can be an overwhelming topic for many, she is audaciously passionate about creating confidence, a sense of security and peace when it comes to their financial well-being.

As a result of learning money smarts early on, she has also made it her mission to teach teens and young adults about money. Through her various workshops, speaking at schools and online education courses, she loves watching the faces light up when they "get it."

With over 35 years working in various roles within the corporate banking arena, including 17 years as a Mortgage Consultant, Patti has a keen and vast understanding of the banking, mortgage and financial industries.

In addition to being a Wealth Advisor, she holds a California Real Estate Brokers license, is a CTA Certified Life Coach and received her Executive Coach

Certification through Marshall Goldsmith Stakeholder Centered Coaching. This unique combination of education and work experience allows Patti to understand her clients from a holistic perspective.

Patti earned her Bachelors of Science degree in Accounting Theory from California State University, Northridge. Patti calls Valencia her home, but the beach is her happy place. She is a single mom to an amazing son, one who inspires her every day. If she isn't enjoying time with family and friends, which she considers her greatest blessings, you can find her at the gym or devouring a book. Full disclosure, she is a self-proclaimed chocoholic.

She is a published author of four books, most recently, *Money Rules 101, Master Your Money Before it Masters You.*

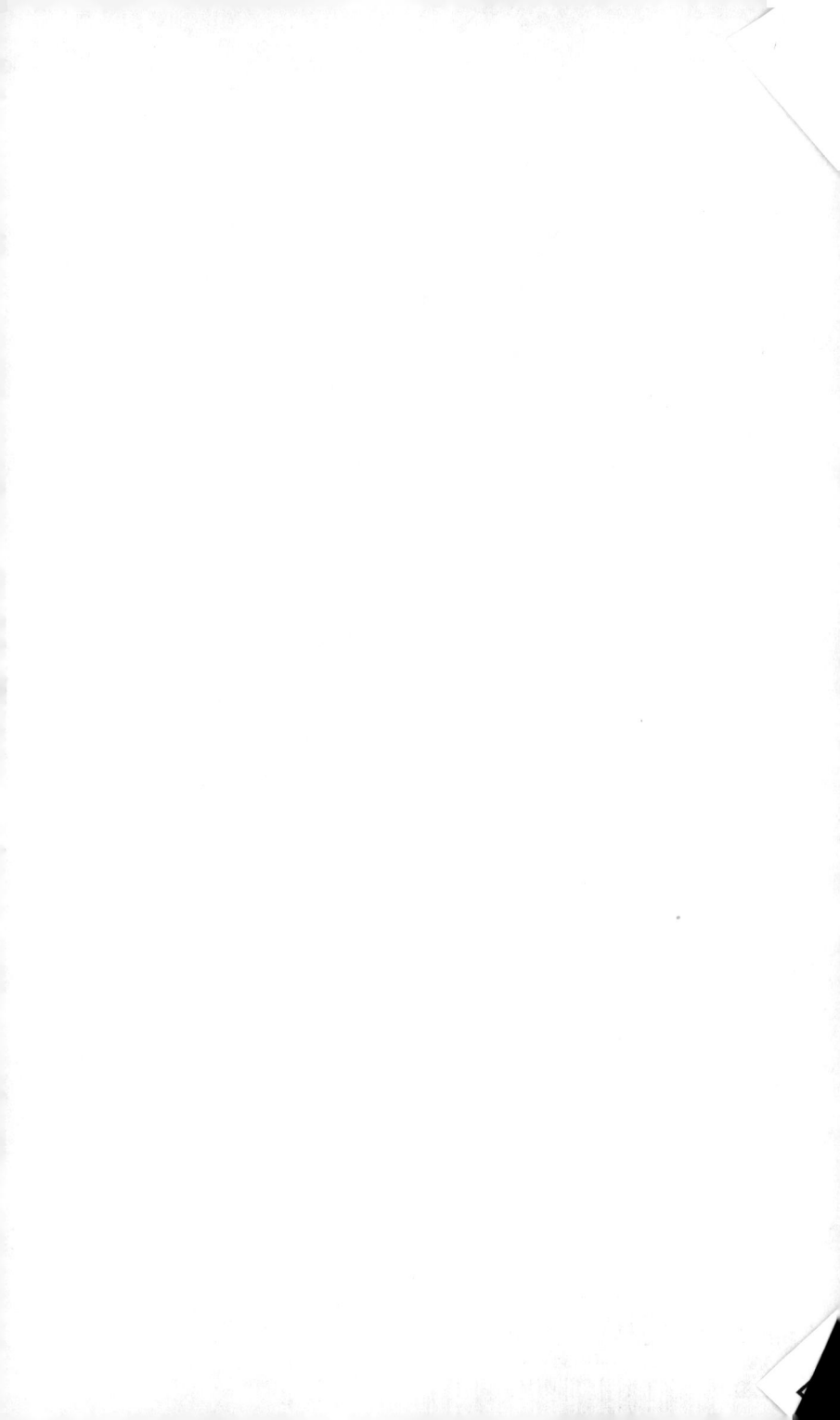